THE GREATEST
OF THESE . . .

THE GREATEST

OF THESE ...

Jane Merchant

A B I N G D O N   P R E S S

New York   *Nashville*

THE GREATEST OF THESE . . .

Library of Congress Catalog Card Number: 54-9197

E

SET UP, PRINTED, AND BOUND BY THE
PARTHENON PRESS, AT NASHVILLE,
TENNESSEE, UNITED STATES OF AMERICA

PREFACE

᠁◦᠁

Ever since I learned to read, from a book of children's verse, I have been reading and memorizing poems and, since I was fourteen, trying to write them. My earliest poetic efforts I contributed to the wastepaper basket, but since 1945, when a sonnet of mine won an award in a farm magazine poetry contest, several hundred of my verses have appeared in various magazines.

One of the poems I memorized earliest, and the one that has meant the most to me, is Paul's "hymn to love" in I Corinthians 13. In using it as the theme of this book, I have tried to share with others both the comfort and the challenge that Paul's words have always been to me. It is my earnest hope that these poems and prayers may help to deepen the reader's responsiveness to the love of God, and to others' need of love in daily living.

This book is dedicated, in loving gratitude, to my mother.

JANE MERCHANT

Many of the poems in this book have appeared previously in periodicals. Acknowledgment is here expressed to the publishers who have graciously permitted their inclusion in this book.

To *Adult Bible Class* for "The Bethlehem Innkeeper's Wife," "Bright Day," "Cause," "For Many Maimed," "In All I Do," "Mary and Martha," "Nothing Lovelier," "Prayer for a Child," "Purchase," "The Shadow," "Teacher of Love," "That We May Sing," "Thy Kingdom Come," "Thy Love Shines Forth," "Understanding," and "The Visible Sign."

To *The Canadian Home Journal* for "The Savers."

To *The Christian Family* for "Sky Lover."

To *The Christian Home* for "Design for Friendship," "Not to the Swift," and "Realities."

To *The Church School* for "Ascent," "Before Gethsemane," "Beyond the Star," "Good Friday," "Interpretation," and "Quiet Things."

To *Classmate* for "Evensong" and "Partnership, Limited."

To *The Farm Journal* for "One Day for Thanks" and "Thanksgiving Table."

To *Household* for "Forever in Their Hearts."

To *The Progressive Farmer* for "For Loveliness."

To *Quiet Hour* for "The Beauty of the Whole," "He Is Risen," and "Thirst."

To *The Saturday Evening Post* for "Afterward," "The Fields of Home," "First Plowing in the Hills," "For My Father," "Grandmother's Message," "Growing Days," "Lanterns and Lamps," "New Neighbor," "Outlander," "Summer Day," and "Winter Trees."

To *Sunday Digest* for "Lesson from Luke."

To *Sunday School Adults* for "Give Them to God."

To *These Times* for "If for One Day," "Of Prayer," and "Thanks for All."

To *Upward* for "April Song," "October Song," "Prayer for Silence," "To Love a Mountain," "Wayfaring Song," and "With Quickening Sight."

To *The War Cry* for "Lesson."

To the *Washington Star* for "Heirloom," "A New House Must Have Love," "Not Yet," and "Song Before Meeting."

To *Youth* for "But Not Too Well," "No Fallacy," and "The Willow Road."

CONTENTS

ﾚﾆﾌﾞﾆﾌﾞﾆ

I. If I Have Not Love

II. A More Excellent Way

III. Love Is Patient and Kind

CONTENTS

IV. Love Never Ends

THE GREATEST OF THESE . . .

I. IF I HAVE NOT LOVE

If I speak in the tongues of men and of angels, but have not love, I am a noisy gong or a clanging cymbal. And if I have prophetic powers, and understand all mysteries and all knowledge, and if I have all faith, so as to remove mountains, but have not love, I am nothing. If I give away all I have, and if I deliver my body to be burned, but have not love, I gain nothing.

—I Cor. 13:1-3

IF I HAVE NOT LOVE

Men send their speech across blue miles of space,
Across great continents their words ring clear,
Yet all their eloquence does not efface
The mountain barriers of hate and fear.
Men chart the heavens' mysteries, have explained
The atom, given their bodies to be burned
In war's fierce hells; and yet have never gained
The good for which their hearts have always yearned.

And I—ah, well indeed, dear Lord, I know
That all that I can say, or think, or do
Is utter nothingness, an idle show,
If I have not deep love, sincere and true;
Love for thy loveliness in star and tree,
Love for my fellow men, pure love for thee.

O Father in heaven, fill our lives with love for thee and for our fellow men. Help us, Lord, to remember always that the healing of a loveless world must begin in our own hearts. Help each of us to strive humbly for honest love in every thought and act. O God of perfect love, teach us to love. In Christ's name. AMEN.

11

With their lips they show much love, but their heart is set on their gain.
—Ezek. 33:31

AS NOISY GONGS

We seek for peace and brotherhood,
Yet war and violence remain.
Though with our lips we show much love,
Our hearts are set upon our gain.

We quibble over ships and price
When starving nations need our grain.
Though with our lips we show much love,
Our hearts are set upon our gain.

We worship God, but not together
With those whose color we disdain.
Though with our lips we show much love,
Our hearts are set upon our gain.

We give our goods to feed the poor,
But not our hearts to share their pain.
Though with our lips we show much love,
Our hearts are set upon our gain.

O holy Master, Lord of love,
Save us from hearing truth in vain.
Teach thou our lives to show much love
And turn our hearts from our own gain.

R 273

O Lord of love, forgive us that we call thee Lord and do not the things that thou sayest. Save us from thinking there is any gain for us apart from thy will. In Christ's name. AMEN.

Let love be genuine; hate what is evil, hold fast to what is good; love one another with brotherly affection; outdo one another in showing honor. Never flag in zeal, be aglow with the Spirit, serve the Lord. Rejoice in your hope, be patient in tribulation, be constant in prayer. —Rom. 12:9-12

WITH ALL WE ARE

We pray with all we are.
We pray with all our hate
As well as all our love.
Our angers, small and great,

And envyings, are heard
Louder than any word,
And often may defeat
The good that we entreat.

We pray with all we are—
Lord, teach us how to pray
In spirit and in truth,
Living the words we say.

O God of truth, forgive us that we sometimes pray for brotherly love without being willing to renounce our petty grudges. Forgive us that we pray for patience and yet try to escape from situations where patience is needed. Help us, Lord, who so much need **thy** help, both to pray and to live in the spirit of Christ. AMEN.

13

He also told this parable to some who trusted in themselves that they were righteous and despised others: "Two men went up into the temple to pray, one a Pharisee and the other a tax collector. The Pharisee stood and prayed thus with himself, 'God, I thank thee that I am not like other men, extortioners, unjust, adulterers, or even like this tax collector.' "   —Luke 18:9-11

LESSON

That I should love my neighbor as myself
Was pure impossibility, I said.
How love one so completely lost to good,
Whose bitter temper was a thing to dread?

He may have lacked much opportunity
To learn good ways to shape his living by,
But with his glaring follies and his faults
How could he claim the love of such as I?

But then I glimpsed how I must look to God,
And now I go about my little labor
Of love, in overwhelmed astonishment
That God should love me as he loves my neighbor.

O God, in mercy deliver us from the self-righteousness that despises others. Make us see ourselves as we are in thy sight, that in humility we may confess our faults and feel compassion for the faults of others. In the name of the compassionate Christ we pray. Amen.

Bear one another's burdens, and so fulfil the law of Christ.
—Gal. 6:2

NOT YET

"I've trouble enough,"
Old Flint will say.
"I can't be going
Out of my way
To help somebody."
And it's quite true
He has had many
A grief to rue.

But since the use
Of trouble should be
To teach one kindness
And sympathy,
And he goes his own way,
Untaught and gruff,
I'd say he hasn't
Had trouble enough.

Father in heaven, grant that we may never be so absorbed in our own troubles that we become indifferent to the troubles of others. Keep us, even in our darkest times, responsive to the needs of other people, and ready to do our utmost to help them, for their sake and for our Master's sake. In his name. AMEN.

Truly, I say to you, as you did it not to one of the least of these, you did it not to me. —Matt. 25:45

THE BETHLEHEM INNKEEPER'S WIFE

What could I do? The house was full of guests,
And each one, wanting everything at once,
Keeping me rushing all day with requests
For this and that. The maid's a witless dunce—
I have to watch her every single minute—
And there's the baby. I finished David's wee
New robe at last, and he looks darling in it.
I couldn't neglect my own child, you'll agree!

But still, I really meant to go to her
And take her some of David's castoff clothes,
She'd have been glad to have, poor as they were.
She was so young! I'm sorry, goodness knows,
She had no woman's comfort. It's too bad.
I really meant to go. . . . I wish I had.

O God our Father, keep our love for our own families from becoming selfish love. Grant that our thoughts and efforts may not be confined to those of our own household, but may include all who are in need of our help. Save us, we pray, from confusion of values, lest in our haste we miss our greatest chance of serving thee. In the name of the Child of Bethlehem. AMEN.

I was a stranger and you did not welcome me.—Matt. 25:43

OUTLANDER

"I thought someone was knocking." She stood eager
As anyone can be who's almost lost
The use of hope, holding the warped door open—
The door with its clean threshold still uncrossed,
After long months, by any foot but hers—
Speaking to silence, as the lonely will
Who listen for replies that never come.
She saw the houses tumbling down the hill
And women talking in the yard nearby.
She stared at them. One turned away her head,
And then they turned around and went inside.
"It must have been the wind. Of course," she said.
"It must have been." And then she flung the door
Wide open, bowing to the icy blast
That rushed into the room. "Come right on in,"
She said to it. "I'm glad you've come at last.
Now sit right down and make yourself at home.
This chair's the best one. Let me fix a cup
Of something hot to warm you. It's cold out.
Yes, it's too cold now, but it may warm up.
It may warm up someday." She wasn't crying.
It was too late. She just sat talking there
And talking to the wind. Cold as it was,
It was her warmest neighbor anywhere.

Our heavenly Father, forgive us for our coldness to those who seem different from us. Forbid that we should ever let any stranger among us perish in spirit for lack of human fellowship. For the sake of Christ our Lord. AMEN.

He giveth to all life, and breath, and all things; and hath made of one blood all nations of men for to dwell on all the face of the earth. —Acts 17:25-26, K.J.V.

DARKNESS

The sun rose in the sky again this morning.
Sometimes I wonder why it wants to rise
And look at all the wrongs it has to see.
Perhaps it doesn't want to, and can't help it,
The way white people don't want—I suppose—
To be unkind, and yet can't seem to help it.
    No, nothing happened, more than usual.
I hunted for a decent place to live
And found a shanty—fit for us, they said.
White people went by in a shiny car.
I heard one say, "They're almost animals
To live like this. Oh, well, I guess they like it."
I wonder if he really thinks we like it.
    We'll move next week. We'll move into the shanty
And leave the willow tree where mockingbirds
Sing songs for us as if our skin were white.
The schools are better there, or so they say.
They can't be worse, at least, and Jimmy's smart.
Don't know if being smart will help him any,
But if there's any chance, he's got to have it.
    Sometimes I think there isn't any chance.
Sometimes I press the darkness to my eyes
And wonder why the sun would want to rise.

Father in heaven, enlighten the darkness of all hearts that despise others for their color or their race. In Christ's name. AMEN.

18

*If you really fulfil the royal law, according to the scripture, "You
shall love your neighbor as yourself," you do well. But if you show
partiality, you commit sin, and are convicted by the law as trans-
gressors. For whoever keeps the whole law but fails in one point
has become guilty of all of it.* —Jas. 2:8-10

THE SHADOW

I have not been unkind, in all my days—
Dear Lord, I have not meant to be unkind—
To any colored person, ever. My ways
Have seldom crossed theirs, but within my mind
And heart I have acknowledged brotherhood
With folk of every race and every hue,
Knowing, since God is Father and all good,
No other faith can possibly be true.

I have not been unkind. But when I see
And hear Miranda's greeting, warm and strong,
There falls between her gentle face and me
The shadow of an immemorial wrong,
And at her smile I feel my spirit wilt
Beneath a withering, suffocating guilt.

Heavenly Father, Father of all human beings everywhere, make us
understand that merely not being unkind is not enough. Make
us realize that we are guilty in thy sight till people of every race
have equal opportunity to live, and laugh, and learn, and to grow
unhindered by prejudice into the fulness of their human possi-
bilities. In Christ's name. AMEN.

19

He is our peace, who has made us both one, and has broken down the dividing wall of hostility.   —Eph. 2:14

PARTNERSHIP, LIMITED

I seldom cross my neighbor's lawn,
He seldom crosses mine,
But every day a crimson bird
Flouts the dividing line,

Plundering sunflower seed from him
And cornbread crumbs from me,
Scattering music about, with blithe
Impartiality.

The gate is shut between us,
The fence is firm and strong,
But we, who live divided, share
Part ownership in song.

Help us, our Father, to work with thy Spirit to break down the walls of hostility and misunderstanding that divide thy children. Make us eager to share with all people the good things thou hast given us. And guard us, Lord, from assuming that any people can have nothing worth while to share with us; make us willing both to give and to receive, that there may be enriching fellowship. In the name of Christ, who is our peace, we pray. AMEN.

II. A More Excellent Way

Are all apostles? Are all prophets? Are all teachers? Do all work miracles? Do all possess gifts of healing? Do all speak with tongues? Do all interpret? But earnestly desire the higher gifts.

And I will show you a still more excellent way.

—I Cor. 12:29-31

A MORE EXCELLENT WAY

Not all possess the ministry of speech,
The blessing of the fitly spoken word;
Not all have wisdom given them, to teach
Eternal truths that have inspired and stirred
Men's hearts through all the centuries; not all
Have gifts of healing mercies in their hands,
Nor faith enough to move a mountain's tall
Relentless barricade from where it stands.

Yet those who lack these gifts are not bereft.
They are good gifts, to be desired, but they
Are not the best; the Lord of love has left
Open to all a still more excellent way;
For anyone, taught by the grace above,
At any time, in any place, may love.

Our heavenly Father, we thank thee that thou art eternally the God of love, and that the poorest and least gifted of us may respond to thy love and learn to love with all our heart and soul and strength and mind. Make us, we pray, creators with thee of the love the world desperately needs. Through Christ our Lord. AMEN.

Behold, a lawyer stood up to put him to the test, saying, "Teacher, what shall I do to inherit eternal life?" He said to him, "What is written in the law? How do you read?" And he answered, "You shall love the Lord your God with all your heart, and with all your soul, and with all your strength, and with all your mind; and your neighbor as yourself." And he said to him, "You have answered right; do this, and you will live." —Luke 10:25-28

DO THIS AND LIVE

The lawyer answered well; he knew the law,
His mind was quick, his comprehension keen.
Unless he loved his neighbor, whom he saw,
He could not love God, whom he had not seen.
So he did not engage in mental labor
On what it means to love the Lord; he tried
Instead to choose just who should be his neighbor,
Lest he might feel himself unjustified.

The lawyer answered well; and well indeed
Christ answered him; unless he proved a friend
By showing love to anyone in need,
His answers would not answer in the end.
No man was ever saved by what he knew.
"Do this and live," He said, and, "Go and do."

Help us, heavenly Father, to fulfill thy law of love. Forgive us that we limit our love and helpfulness to those who love us, to those who are like ourselves. Preserve us from knowing to do good and doing it not. In the name of Christ, who went about doing good. AMEN.

Love does no wrong to a neighbor; therefore love is the fulfilling of the law. —Rom. 13:10

NEW NEIGHBOR

I do not ask your friendship; friendship grows
From closer causes than proximity.
The spirit's promontories and plateaus
Are not determined by geography,
And you and I may share this hilltop weather,
This winding street, for years, and never find
The quiet way by which friends meet together
In the intrinsic climate of the mind.

But there is pleasant comradeship in sharing
Familiar scenes of living, day by day,
And in exchanging generous, unsparing
Kind acts of helpfulness, as neighbors may,
And these I offer, grateful if it should
Prove we may share the heart's own neighborhood.

II. A More Excellent Way

We thank thee, gracious Father, for good neighbors, whose thoughtful words and acts add to our happiness each day. Help us to be such neighbors, Lord, as we are glad to have. Help us to offer every neighbor, whatever his attitude toward us may be, unfailing good will and creative sympathy. In Christ's name. Amen.

I have called you friends.—John 15:15

DESIGN FOR FRIENDSHIP

Let there be wonder always, and a shared
Delight in constant growing toward the best,
In books and thoughts examined and compared
With eager curiosity and zest.
Let there be laughter, and the interchange
Of glad experience enriching each
With double joy, as there must be the range
Of understanding only tears can teach.

And let there be continuous deepening
Of love in fruitful silences, whereby
Each heart communicates the urgent thing
That each heart must communicate, or die.
And you shall learn in this way, and no other,
Friendship is hearts refreshing one another.

O thou our greatest Friend, we thank thee for the friends thou
hast given us, whose enthusiasm for the good inspires our minds
and whose tender understanding sustains our hearts. We thank thee
for enriching experiences of joy and sorrow shared. Help us, dear
Lord, to be more worthy of our friends. In Christ's name. AMEN.

SONG BEFORE MEETING

I hope you're thinking of me
In everything you do,
And finding time to love me
As I am loving you.

I hope anticipation
Of moments we shall spend
In such good conversation
As friend may have with friend

Makes all your work seem lighter,
Makes all your care seem less,
And gives a gayer, brighter
Glow to each small success.

I hope that when we've parted
Reluctantly, you'll go
Refreshed and happier hearted
With faith renewed; for so

I'll know that I am giving
To you, in some degree,
The deepened joy in living
That you have given me.

We thank thee, Lord, for good hours spent wtih friends whose presence refreshes us in heart and mind, whose faith renews our own. Help us to transfer to everyone we meet something of the tenderness we feel for those who are especially dear to us, that our love for family and friends may bless all whose lives touch ours. In Christ's name. AMEN.

Let us not love in word or speech but in deed and in truth.
—I John 3:18

TEACHER OF LOVE

My mother taught me love; the love of high
Blue hills, the love of starlight and of rain,
The constant, changeless love of earth and sky,
The love of singing words, the love of plain
Sincerity and truth in act and thought,
The love of service and of helpfulness,
The love of honest work, securely wrought,
And fortitude undaunted by distress.

My mother taught deep, lasting love to me
Of all things good and beautiful, with no
Great need of words, since love and bravery
And beauty and integrity are so
Much part of all her life and character
I learned the love of them, in loving her.

Father of love, giver of every good and perfect gift, most fervently
we thank thee for those whose lives have taught us love. Words
cannot speak our gratitude to thee and to them for all they have
meant to us. Help us, dear Lord, to live our gratitude. Help us to
practice love as they have practiced it. In Christ's name. AMEN.

Come away by yourselves to a lonely place, and rest a while.
—Mark 6:31

GROWING DAYS

"You've had as much excitement as you should,"
Our mother very often used to say.
"The fun you've had won't do you any good
Till it has settled down in you to stay.
Go listen to the creek and nibble cress,
Go count the grass and catch up to your living."
So we would revel in green idleness
And never realize what she was giving;

A chance to savor new experience slowly
And thoroughly, assimilating all
Its deep significance, till it was wholly
Our own past any possible recall.
"No use to give them things," she always knew,
"Unless you give them time to keep them, too."

Our Father, who in thy loving wisdom hast ordained days of rest for us, help us to remember our need, throughout our lives, for time alone to renew our strength, and to become more nearly what thou wouldst have us be. Keep us always, Lord, from the unthinking haste that makes for shallow souls and trivial service. In the name of Christ, who sought the lonely places. AMEN.

For thus said the Lord God, the Holy One of Israel,
  "In returning and rest you shall be saved;
    in quietness and in trust shall be your strength."
And you would not, but you said,
"No! We will speed upon horses,"
    therefore you shall speed away.

—Isa. 30:15-16

NOT TO THE SWIFT

Men thundering through the firmament,
On saving seconds grimly bent,
Have never time to pause and stare
At white birds arching down blue air;

And, hurtling headlong over earth
To earn an extra moment's mirth,
Have never time to understand
Long rhythms of the rolling land;

Have never time enough to gaze
At hills serene in smoky haze,
Nor ever time to stop and see
Green wisdom in a blowing tree.

They squander suns to save a day,
In hoarding nights, fling stars away,
And, in their hot pursuit of haste,
Let earth and heaven run to waste.

O God of returning and rest, heal us of our feverish ways. Forgive us that we sometimes seek in ceaseless activity to escape from ourselves, and from thee. Give us wisdom and grace to be still, to look with seeing eyes upon thy world, and to lift our hearts in gratitude to thee. AMEN.

A workman made it;
it is not God.
—Hos. 8:6

TEXT FOR TODAY

"A workman made it; it is not God."
These surely are needless words today.
We worship no idols of silver or gold
Or images fashioned of wood or clay.

Yet "a workman made it; it is not God."
Over and over the warning rings.
Do we work for God as we work to earn
The means of purchasing man-made things?

Do we seek for God as we seek for gain?
Is our standard of living truly high,
Or is it merely a standard of having,
Based on the things we are able to buy?

These words that were spoken ages ago
Are ours to use as a measuring rod
For all that science and industry do:
"A workman made it; it is not God."

Forgive us, O God, for our too-great reliance on comforts and conveniences and pleasures. Guard us from exhausting our energies and dulling ourselves for thy service in our eagerness to acquire material things. And save us always, Lord, from basing our hope for a better world on the products of men's minds and hands, instead of on the waking of thy Spirit in men's hearts. In Christ's name. AMEN.

Whatever is true, whatever is honorable, whatever is just, whatever is pure, whatever is lovely, whatever is gracious, if there is any excellence, if there is anything worthy of praise, think about these things. —Phil. 4:8

QUIET THINGS

He is at peace who cherishes delight
In quiet things;
In the enchanted hush of trees where white
Snow-silence clings,

In the slow arc of one late-homing bird,
Song without sound,
In fields where, safely undiscovered, furred
Small things abound,

In reverential twilight calms, that wait
Star-harmonies,
Pearled mornings, tranquilly inviolate—
Who treasures these

Has infinite resource of loveliness
In his own soul
And shall remain, through turmoil and distress,
Steadfastly whole.

Teach us, O God of all things gracious, pure, and lovely, to think about these things. If there are in our lives unlovely scenes and unjust situations which we cannot change, teach us to think not of them but of the many things that are worthy of praise. Let our minds be so filled with what is excellent and honorable that we may praise, and not complain; appreciate, not criticize. In Christ's name. AMEN.

O give thanks to the Lord, for he is good,
*   for his steadfast love endures for ever.*

. . . .

To him who by understanding made the heavens,
*   for his steadfast love endures for ever;*
to him who spread out the earth upon the waters,
*   for his steadfast love endures for ever;*
to him who made the great lights,
*   for his steadfast love endures for ever.*
                                    —Ps. 136:1, 5-7

THY LOVE SHINES FORTH

Thy world is lovely, Lord,
The gracious fields of green,
The little rains on tender grass
And the dim velvet sheen

Of light on moonstruck trees
Rapt in white dreams of song,
And trees that meet the storm
And laugh into the long

Wild winds, and hills that keep
Eternal tryst with thee.
Thy world is lovely, Lord; thy love
Shines forth in all we see.

O Father of enduring, steadfast love, we thank thee for the beauty of thy world. We marvel at the greatness of thy love, that hast given us so fair a dwelling place, and eyes to see and spirits to respond. Oh, never let our eyes grow blind to beauty, our spirits unresponsive to thy love. In the name of Christ, thy greatest gift of love. AMEN.

And let the beauty of the Lord our God be upon us: and establish thou the work of our hands upon us; yea, the work of our hands establish thou it. —Ps. 90:17, K.J.V.

FOR LOVELINESS

Along with all the beauty of thy world
That thou hast given me, dear Lord, to see,
Along with dawns, and brilliant clouds unfurled
From mountain peaks, and varied artistry
Of shell and spider web to marvel at,
And myriad excellence in shape and hue
Of flower and leaf and wing, my prayer is that
Thou give, as well, some work that I can do.

Some work to do for thee, that shall express
My thanks, as words cannot; the humblest task
May offer gratitude for loveliness,
And since thy world is lovely, I would ask
To work with heart and hand and mind and will
To make it, if I may, more lovely still.

Dear Lord, give each of us sure guidance to the work thou hast appointed for us to do, and let us be willing always to accept thy guidance. Help us to give the smallest, humblest tasks our very best, in joyous gratitude; and if thou givest tasks that seem beyond our powers, help us to undertake them bravely, trusting thee to enable us to do them well. Through Christ our Lord. Amen.

Man goes forth to his work
and to his labor until the evening.
—Ps. 104:23

FIRST PLOWING IN THE HILLS

When it's too soon for spring, and even too soon
To think of it, you'd think—some afternoon
You're sure to raise your eyes and see them there
Cresting the topmost ridge that tries to pare
Whole sections from the sky; a man and team
Of horses plowing. Cloud and clod would seem
To feel the plowshare equally. You wonder
If the sun itself isn't apt to be plowed under
In that steep enterprise. It makes you proud
Of men who'll start out halfway up a cloud
To sketch designs for summer on a land
That isn't sure of spring. You understand,
Of course, it's hard work plowing on a hill,
And bottom lands grow better crops, but still
There's something useful to the heart and eye
In men who plow the earth, against the sky.

We thank thee, our Father, for the faith of those who toil in drought and heat, in rain and cold, that there may be food for us. May thy blessing be upon them, on the fields they till and the seed they sow. Give them joy in labor, and a rich harvest, and, in the evening, quiet rest with thee. In the name of Christ. AMEN.

While the earth remains, seedtime and harvest, cold and heat,
summer and winter, day and night, shall not cease.

—Gen. 8:22

THE FIELDS OF HOME

Our minds retain the contours of the land
That gave us life. These valleys shaped our thought
To their own sweeping rhythms, to reach, expand
To larger distances. These tall hills taught
Our hearts the shape of courage, and we learned
From ample meadows open to the sky
Accepting sun and wind, no influence spurned,
Patterns of breadth to fashion tolerance by.

We garnered faith from every season's sowing,
Hope with each harvest. Far though we may dwell,
Ours the assurance, undismayed by ill,
Of life's long strength, of life's eternal growing.
The fields of home have fed our spirits well
And in all years to come shall feed us still.

Lord of the constant earth and changing seasons, we thank thee for
these ancient certainties. We thank thee for the goodness of the
land that thou hast made, and for all that it has taught us of faith,
and hope, and love. May our lives be like the good soil, Lord,
that brings forth fruit with patience. In Christ's name. AMEN.

I lift up my eyes to the hills.
From whence does my help come?
My help comes from the Lord,
who made heaven and earth.
—Ps. 121:1-2

TO LOVE A MOUNTAIN

There is a mountain far beyond my window,
Oh, infinitely far and far away,
And yet as close against my heart as love is,
As liberal love, enlarging day by day.

To love a mountain is to learn of tallness,
Of quiet strength, forever unsubdued.
To love a mountain is to grow a little
Each time one sees its shining altitude.

It may be, if I love it well enough,
That some day I may journey up the far
Aspiring summit, the attaining height,
And lean my heart at last against a star.

O Thou most high, we praise thee for the blessings of the eternal mountains, for the bounties of the everlasting hills. As thou hast made the mountains strong to endure the fiercest storms, help our hearts to be strong and tranquil in times of stress. As thou hast made the hills lift upward toward the sky, help our hearts rise above our lowlands of defeat and sorrow. In Christ's name. AMEN.

Thy steadfast love, O Lord, extends to the heavens,
thy faithfulness to the clouds.

—Ps. 36:5

SKY LOVER

I have been told of folk who seldom lift
Their eyes from earth's minute preoccupations
Into complete acceptance of the gift
Of sky, who never note its variations
From luminous pearl to azure, with an eye
Experienced in appreciating each
Tranquillity of coloring, who deny
Their thoughts the heaven-given right to reach

After a lonely soaring bird, as far
As love can follow. To know but sun and rain
With an occasional glimpse of moon and star
Is not enough of sky. I would remain
Always entirely, reverently aware
Of all the daily mercies waiting there.

We praise thee, Lord of the heavens, for the great wide grace of
the sky, that rests us from our little daily cares. May we be always
aware of the sky's large depths of tender blue and of its changing
glory of clouds, reading thy messages of love in all. In the name
of Christ. AMEN.

Look at the birds of the air: they neither sow nor reap nor gather into barns, and yet your heavenly Father feeds them. Are you not of more value than they? —Matt. 6:26

WITH QUICKENING SIGHT

I have pursued
With quickening sight
The joyous way
Of a bird in flight;

And, tracing it
Unerringly
To coverture
Of greenery,

Have been somehow
Intensely stirred,
Feeling my heart
Winged like a bird.

Father of bounties, we praise thee for the swift grace of birds that flash across our anxious downcast sight, reminding us of thy perpetual care and bringing sudden gladness to our hearts. We praise thee in Christ's name. AMEN.

The leaves of the tree were for the healing of the nations.
—Rev. 22:2

THE VISIBLE SIGN

I think that trees are love's own loveliness
Made visible. Their leafy rhythmic motion
Contents my spirit like the soft caress
Of one held dear, and wakes my heart's devotion
And gratitude to God for all the grace
Of being, for all holy peace and health
Of soul, like radiance of a well-loved face
Gently bestowing friendship's quiet wealth.

I think that trees are love and hope, the living
Fruition of faith's minutely tiny seed
That from the least becomes the greatest, giving
Gracious fulfillment of our deepest need.
Trees are forever love and faith to me,
Since Christ our Saviour died upon a tree.

We praise thee, heavenly Father, for all trees, which, ever reaching upward, draw our hearts unto thee. We praise thee most of all for the surpassing love of Christ, who died for us upon a tree, that through him we might have healing and the gift of life eternal. We praise thee in his name. AMEN.

Lo, the winter is past,
  the rain is over and gone.
The flowers appear on the earth,
  the time of singing has come.
                    —Song of S. 2:11-12

APRIL SONG

Sing praise to God for April,
For bliss of apple bloom,
For honeysuckle's fragrance,
For lilac's cool perfume,
For dogwood white and holy
Upon a moonlit hill
Where mockingbirds, enchanted,
Glad psalms of rapture spill.

Sing praise to God for April,
For green and silver days
Of shy and tender glories—
Oh, ever sing his praise.
Praise him till praises echo
To the tall blue above
Who clothed the earth with April
And blessed it with his love.

We praise thee, Lord, for the glorious renewal of springtime, which brings fresh hope to weary hearts and minds. Grant that we may look at the gentle, tender glories of the spring days with such perceptive eyes and receiving hearts that their beauty becomes a part of all we are and of all we do. In Christ's name. AMEN.

This is the Lord's doing;
it is marvelous in our eyes.
This is the day which the Lord has made;
let us rejoice and be glad in it.
—Ps. 118:23-24

BRIGHT DAY

This is the day
Which the Lord has made
From dazzle of sun
And dapple of shade,

From joyous green
And rapturous blue
And gold light making
All things new;

A sample of heaven
Floating free
To stay us till
Eternity.

Our heavenly Father, teach us that all our days are days that thou hast made, and that, trusting thee, we may ever be glad and rejoice in them. Help us, Lord, to remember always that nothing comes to us without thy will; help us to perceive thy steadfast love in dark days as well as in bright. In Christ's name. AMEN.

Every day I will bless thee.
—Ps. 145:2

SUMMER DAY

It was an ordinary summer day
With customary opalescent dawn
Shining upon the usual array
Of spider-thread lace scattered on the lawn,
And flowers conventionally bright and gay,
And grass too green to seem entirely true,
And sun proceeding, in the wonted way,
Across a sky of regulation blue.

No songbird uttered any note that I
Had never heard before; sunset perfected
Its common incandescence in the sky,
And stars emerged exactly as expected.
A routine day, when all is said and done—
But I could never ask a lovelier one.

We thank thee, Lord, for all the goodness and all the gaiety of what
we call our ordinary days. We thank thee that our days are in thy
hands, and that thou fillest them with amazing loveliness and with
thy presence above all and in all and through all. We thank thee,
Father, in Christ's name for all the little joys of every day. AMEN.

Let the heavens be glad, and let the earth rejoice;

. . . .

let the field exult, and everything in it!
Then shall all the trees of the wood sing for joy.
—Ps. 96:11-12

OCTOBER SONG

A day of wind and sunshine
And whirling gusts of gold,
And something more of loveliness
Than human hearts can hold.

A day of crimson glories
And tangy tingling air,
And something more of happiness
Than human hearts can bear.

Oh, pure must be his spirit,
His tongue well taught to pray
In gratitude, who can endure
A tall October day.

O God of glory, radiance, and beauty, we thank thee for the bright purity of autumn skies, for the rich, exulting fields, for the colors of the trees that seem to sing aloud for joy. Purify our minds and spirits, Lord; quicken us to live lives more worthy of the glowing wonder of these days. In Christ's name. AMEN.

For everything there is a season, and a time for every matter under heaven:

. . . .

a time to seek, and a time to lose;
a time to keep, and a time to cast away.

—Eccl. 3:1, 6

WINTER TREES

The leafy grace
Of summer wanes
And leaves no trace;
Yet strength remains—

The central strength
That rests content
Through winter's length,
Unlost, unspent.

Who sees them now,
Bereft, unbowed,
Must be somehow
Assured and proud.

A need that green
Could not appease
Feeds on the lean
Undaunted trees.

O God, who hast made trees beautiful in their winter times of loss, help us to remember thy promise that as the days of a tree shall the days of thy people be. Grant, our Father, that in our winter seasons we too may abide unbowed and tranquil, waiting in quietness for the springtime that will surely come. Through Christ our Lord. Amen.

He who does not love remains in death.—I John 3:14

NO FALLACY

Is a bluebird any bluer
Because of weary eyes that treasure
Lifting, lilting sky-winged pleasure
In its flight?

Is a maple any taller
Because of a wounded spirit feeling
Slow serenity of healing
In its shade?

Do not smile at me for asking,
Do not chide me for believing
All things lovelier for receiving
Any love.

Our heavenly Father, grant us unfailing faith in the power of love to overcome all sorrow, all hatred, and all evil. May we never doubt that genuine love can call forth goodness and beauty in the most seemingly unresponsive human heart. Make us pure channels, Lord, through which thy love may reach all those who need it most. In the name of Christ our Lord. AMEN.

III. Love Is Patient and Kind

Love is patient and kind; love is not jealous or boastful; it is not arrogant or rude. Love does not insist on its own way; it is not irritable or resentful; it does not rejoice at wrong, but rejoices in the right. Love bears all things, believes all things, hopes all things, endures all things. —I Cor. 13:4-7

LOVE IS PATIENT AND KIND

But we, who are impatient and unkind
Even when we would not be; we who can bear
So little, in believing hope, are blind
So often, to another's load of care
And irritable beneath our own; and who
Are boastful and resentful, and insist
On having our own way—what shall we do
To find the excellent way that we have missed?

Only by close companionship with One
Who is the Way, who lived all love, who will
Not leave us comfortless, can it be done;
But as we wait before him and are still,
We learn to know that God is love, and thus
At last, we love, because he first loved us.

Lord God of love, thou knowest our hearts and how great are our failures to love. Save us, Lord, from our unloving tempers and from our preoccupation with ourselves. Purify us of all that separates us from thee, and grant us such revealings of thy Spirit that we may share in the love thou hast for every living soul. Through Christ our Lord. Amen.

If you love those who love you, what credit is that to you? . . .
Love your enemies, and do good, and lend, expecting nothing in
return; and your reward will be great, and you will be sons of the
Most High; for he is kind to the ungrateful and the selfish.

—Luke 6:32, 35

WHILE WE PRAY

God does not love as we love; God does not
Love us for any loveliness within
Our hearts and souls; he loves us, knowing what
We are, in all our selfishness and sin.
God does not love us weakly, with a blind
Indulgence; he must change our lives, since he
Is holiness, inexorably kind,
From what they are to what they ought to be.

We love the lovable, the wise, the good,
Those who return our love, those who have done
What we desire; but God's great fatherhood
Loves each ungrateful, selfish, loveless one.
God does not love as we love; but we may
Learn how to love as God loves, while we pray.

We thank thee, O God most high, that thou art kind to the ungrateful and the selfish. Help us to be kind to other ungrateful and
selfish ones, Lord, as thou art kind to us. Help us, who can scarcely
love our friends unselfishly, to love our enemies. Help us to understand the pressures and strains that cause them to do wrong, as
thou understandest ours, and to forgive them, as thou forgivest us.
Through Christ our Lord. AMEN.

GARDEN AT TWILIGHT

Now in this twilight hour,
Rest from your little cares
Among God's growing things,
Where silences are prayers.

Rest from your little cares,
And let God's love expand
Your heart to loving care
For folk in every land.

Among God's growing things,
Pray that God's love may grow
In all hearts everywhere
Beneath the twilight glow.

Where silences are prayers,
Learn, reverently still,
To love the Father's love,
To will the Father's will.

Dear Lord, among the healing peace of growing things we ask thy healing for all sick and weary souls and bodies, thy peace for all confused and troubled minds, thy forgiving love for all resentful, angry spirits. We thank thee, Father, that while we pray for thy blessings upon all people, we may know ourselves at one with thee and with all those in every land who call upon thee in truth. Through Christ our Lord. Amen.

After he had dismissed the crowds, he went up into the hills by himself to pray. When evening came, he was there alone.
—Matt. 14:23

EVENSONG

There is a need for quietness
That evening's hush fulfills
When twilight shadows gently drift
Across the dreaming hills.

There is a peace that satisfies
The spirit's slow desire,
An infinite tranquillity
That weary souls require.

And there is reverence and faith
No crowded noon can cheapen.
Oh, keep an hour for quietness
While the dim shadows deepen.

O God and Father of our Lord Jesus Christ, help us to learn from him our need to be alone at evening, to pray. As he did not rely on his own strength apart from thee, so we would not rely on our own. We thank thee for the quietness of evening, that rests us from the burden of the day. We thank thee for thy presence, restoring our souls. AMEN.

The whole earth is at rest and quiet;
they break forth into singing.
Isa. 14:7

THAT WE MAY SING

Thou art not far from any one of us,
However far we are, O Lord, from thee.
Give us the grace of quietness, to know
Thy presence and thy holy harmony

Within our hearts through all the hurried hours,
Through all the clamorous din of busy days,
Till in the listening silence of our souls
There stirs a song of worship and of praise,

A song of praise to thee for all thy love,
A song of love for every living thing
That thou, our Father and our God, hast made.
O teach us to be still, that we may sing.

We thank thee, Lord, for times when we are hushed and still before thee, when we have rest from our own clamorous desires, and all our will becomes obedient to thy will. We thank thee for the wonder of these hours, when thy Spirit liberates us from ourselves. Forgive us that these hours come seldom, that we do not always wait patiently for thee, so that our hearts grow dull and lose their song. We pray in Christ's name. AMEN.

LITTLE SONGS

I'm glad the Father never asks
That all of us who raise
Our songs to him, at common tasks,
Should adequately praise

His glorious name, with pealing notes
Of anthems nobly soaring,
Or that we voice, with faultless throats,
Our souls' sincere adoring.

Although our music be subdued,
Our God is listening
To little songs of gratitude
That anyone can sing.

Our Father, we thank thee that thou hearest all our attempts to praise thee. We would praise thee not only with our songs but also with our service, never neglecting to use whatever talent we possess, however small, through fear that it may not be worthy of thee. In Christ's name. AMEN.

We know that in everything God works for good with those who love him, who are called according to his purpose.

—Rom. 8:28

OF PRAYER

How strange that anyone should claim the key
To prayer, how strange that anyone should say
Petitions voiced in any certain way,
In any certain mood, will surely be
Productive of the one result desired.
Can anyone presume that God will do
Precisely what some human asks him to
Because his prayer method is inspired?

The heart of faith that trusts that God is love
And that his will for us is always good
Waits, certain of its answer from above
In secret ways, not seen or understood,
And this may be the best and surest prayer:
To lift each need to God, and leave it there.

Father in heaven, give us hearts of faith to trust in thy love, and to trust thy wisdom more than our own, believing faithfully that thou wilt fulfill all our good desires in thy own time and way. Thou knowest all our needs; thou knowest we have need of many things. But teach us that our greatest need is for the constant realization of thy presence. In Christ's name. AMEN.

Cast all your anxieties on him, for he cares about you.
—I Pet. 5:7

GIVE THEM TO GOD

God needs the lonely places in your heart,
God needs the desolate, the unshared hours
Of loss and pain and friends' misunderstanding,
The weary hours when all your strength is spent
And all your wisdom is not wise enough.

Give them to him, the hurt, forsaken hours.
He will receive them lovingly, and give
What you at last are ready to receive,
The fullness of his comfort and his grace,
The encompassing presence of his love.

God needs the hours you know your need of him,
The lonely places only he can fill.

Forgive us, Lord, that it is often only after we have exhausted all
other resources that we turn our hearts entirely unto thee. Forgive
us that we seek from friends the help that only thou canst give,
and that we grow bitter, believing that they have failed us, when
it is we who have failed thee. Teach us, our Father, to bring all
our sorrows and failures to thee, that thou mayst show us our
errors and console and strengthen us. In Christ's name. AMEN.

The Spirit helps us in our weakness; for we do not know how to pray as we ought, but the Spirit himself intercedes for us with sighs too deep for words.—Rom. 8:26

FOR LOVED ONES

I know not what to pray for as I should,
Dear Lord, for friends who are in need of thee,
But as I bless them all, and will their good,
I know thou knowest their needs, Lord, and wilt be
To them far more than I can think or ask,
Out of the great abundance of thy grace
Giving them strength and courage for each task,
Making them adequate for their own place.

So, Lord of generous mercies, throned above,
I name their names to thee, that thou mayst bless
Each one of them according to thy love,
According to thy righteous tenderness,
Trusting that each of them, Lord, hour by hour,
May know thy peace, thy presence, and thy power.

As we remember our loved ones in thy presence, Lord, holding them before thee in our hearts, we thank thee for them all. We pray that thou wilt cleanse our love for them of all selfishness and all possessiveness. Help us, since we desire their good, always to be sympathetic and understanding with them, and never thoughtlessly to hurt them in any way. In Christ's name. AMEN.

Set a guard over my mouth, O Lord,
keep watch over the door of my lips!
—Ps. 141:3

PRAYER FOR SILENCE

Give me the gift of silence, Lord,
The grace of keeping still
Whenever anything I say
Might work another's ill.

I've said so many foolish things
In idle, aimless chatter,
I've spoken sharp, impulsive words
As if it didn't matter

How much I hurt another's heart—
Lord, keep me still, I pray.
I've seldom had to be ashamed
Of words I didn't say.

O God, who hast given us families and friends to love and cherish, forgive us that we wound them and ourselves by our sudden irritabilities, our unconsidered speech. Help us to be gentle and thoughtful always, that we may guard our tongues and spare the hearts of those who love us and whom we love. In the name of Christ. AMEN.

Then children were brought to him that he might lay his hands on them and pray. The disciples rebuked the people; but Jesus said, "Let the children come to me, and do not hinder them; for to such belongs the kingdom of heaven." —Matt. 19:13-14

PRAYER FOR A CHILD

O Father, let him love the rain,
And stars, and sun, and solitude,
And fields of blowing golden grain,
And fields of autumn, quiet hued.

And let him love all leafless trees
Creating grace from barrenness,
And leafy treasuries of peace
The slow green winds of summer bless.

Give him a heart that soars and sings
In gratitude; O hear my plea
That all beloved and lovely things
Lead him to larger love of thee.

We thank thee, our Father, that the children who are dear to us are dearer still to thee. We thank thee for Christ's blessing on the children, and we pray thy blessing on all children everywhere. Help us, we pray, to build a world where children may grow joyously, in love, not warped in soul and body by hunger, strife, and fear. In Christ's name. AMEN.

Pray at all times in the Spirit, with all prayer and supplication.
—Eph. 6:18

THY KINGDOM COME

For all who pass by,
For the boy on his bike,
For the slovenly woman
With the curly-haired tyke,

For the hungry-eyed couple,
Luxuriously clad,
For the ragged street cleaner
And the boy with his dad;

For all who pass by,
O Father, I pray
Thy will be done
In them today.

O God of compassion and mercy, be with all people, we pray, and bless them according to thy knowledge of their needs. Incline the hearts of all people to seek thee, that thy will, which is forever good, may be done in them and through them, for the coming of thy kingdom. In Christ's name. AMEN.

Blessed be the God and Father of our Lord Jesus Christ, the Father of mercies and God of all comfort, who comforts us in all our affliction, so that we may be able to comfort those who are in any affliction, with the comfort with which we ourselves are comforted by God.
—II Cor. 1:3-4

UNDERSTANDING

We who live with longing
For what can never be
May have a more perceptive
Responsive sympathy

With others' aspirations
Than those who never know
The weight of hopeless longing
That clogs the heart; and though

We cannot grant fulfillment
Of yearning—while we live,
The gift of understanding
Is always ours to give.

Father of mercies, God of all comfort, help us by thy grace to use all the sorrow of our lives that it may make us gentle and compassionate. Let the loneliness of losing what we love teach us how great others' loneliness may be, and how deep their need of one who understands and cares. Help us, dear Lord, to understand and care. In Christ's name. AMEN.

Truly, I say to you, whoever gives you a cup of water to drink because you bear the name of Christ, will by no means lose his reward. —Mark 9:41

THIRST

Why does he come so often to her door,
The weary, bent old man who mows the grass,
To ask, as if he had not asked before
Not quite ten minutes earlier, for a glass
Of water? Mowing lawns is thirsty work,
And yet it is not only thirst, I think,
Nor, surely, any least desire to shirk,
That makes him come so often for a drink.

Perhaps he knows but few who would not scold,
Who would not grow impatient now and then,
Who would not fail to have the water cold
When he comes back again and yet again.
Perhaps he knows how hard it is to find
Someone who is completely, wholly kind.

Our Father, help us to be kind in all our relationships, even when the ways of being kind may seem too small to matter. Help us to look beyond the seemingly unreasonable demands of others to the search for reassurance which such demands may represent. Grant, Lord, that we may fear being imposed upon less than we fear imposing our impatience on a heart that may already be bearing all that it can bear. In Christ's name. AMEN.

Put on then, as God's chosen ones, holy and beloved, compassion, kindness, lowliness, meekness, and patience, forbearing one another and, if one has a complaint against another, forgiving each other; as the Lord has forgiven you, so you also must forgive. And above all these put on love, which binds everything together in perfect harmony. —Col. 3:12-14

HEIRLOOM

The cup my great-grandmother brought
A thousand miles or more
To make a home of wilderness
Lies broken on the floor.

The fragile, gently cherished cup
From which she drank delight
Lies broken by a careless girl
Who looks at me in fright.

My great-grandmother was too kind
For any heart to shatter
About her cup; I smile, and say,
"My dear, it doesn't matter."

We know, Lord, that we must forgive the greatest wrongs that others do us; help us to know that we must forgive the least. Help us to live always in the consciousness of thy forgiving love, that we may not be suddenly betrayed into ungentle, unforgiving speech or action. In our Saviour's name. AMEN.

*Whatever you wish that men would do to you, do so to them;
for this is the law and the prophets.*   —Matt. 7:12

PURCHASE

I almost bought a dozen combs today,
A dozen combs I didn't need at all,
Because the thin boy offering the array,
At the back door, of various large and small
Combs of all kinds and colors, when I said,
"Good morning," showed me, with a resolute
White face, a narrow card on which I read
The neatly lettered words, "I'm deaf and mute."

A thrush was singing then. I would have bought
His whole supply, but that his look forbade
My charity; so after careful thought
I took just one, the finest one he had.
I could not sleep tonight if I had tried
To buy his courage of him, and his pride.

O Father of compassionate understanding, give us imaginative sympathy and warmth of heart to enter into the feelings of others.
Let us never offer other people the pity that we would not accept
ourselves, that would destroy their self-respect. Lord, help us to
give, rather, the compassion that helps them to help themselves. In
the name of Christ. AMEN.

Let all bitterness and wrath and anger and clamor and slander be put away from you, with all malice, and be kind to one another, tenderhearted, forgiving one another, as God in Christ forgave you.
—Eph. 4:31-32

LEST I LOSE

If there is anger in my heart,
I cannot see
The beauty of wind-rippled leaves
On any tree.

If there is envy in my heart,
I have no eyes
For the beauty of white wind-blown clouds
In any skies.

Lord, keep me gentle, keep me still,
Lord, keep me kind,
Lest I lose all thy loveliness,
Lest I be blind.

O merciful Father, thou knowest how quickly we forget, in a moment's blinding anger, our good resolves and our sense of thy immediate loving nearness. Grant us sincere repentance for our dishonorings of thee by wrath and bitterness. Save us from despair of ever overcoming our little daily sins. Help us, each time we fail, to ask thy pardon instantly, and to persevere in trying to do better. Through Christ our Lord. AMEN.

The fruit of the Spirit is love, joy, peace, patience, kindness, goodness, faithfulness, gentleness, self-control; against such there is no law.—Gal. 5:22-23

THAT I MAY GIVE

Lord, knowing how I fail
To give unsparingly
The love I owe to others,
The help and sympathy,

Let me not be resentful
When others fail to give
The understanding love
I need to help me live.

Help me to turn, instead,
My soul to thee; O feed
My hungry heart, that I may give
To others all I need.

Father of great and generous giving, we pray for thy spirit of generosity to enter into and take possession of our spirits. We would be generous in our giving, and above all generous in our thoughts of those to whom we give, even if they sometimes seem thoughtless and ungrateful. We pray in the name of Christ, who gave his life for us. AMEN.

O Lord, who shall sojourn in thy tent?
  Who shall dwell on thy holy hill?

He who walks blamelessly, and does what is right,
  and speaks truth from his heart;
who does not slander with his tongue,
  and does no evil to his friend,
    nor takes up a reproach against his neighbor.
                                        —Ps. 15:1-3

INTERPRETATION

To live a life above reproach must mean,
I sometimes think, not merely living so
Upright and virtuous a life that no
Critic can harm us with censorious spleen.
I think it is to keep our minds serene
Above reproachful thoughts of what friends owe
Of thoughtfulness, and fail in; to forego
Nursing our little hurts, however keen.

For much tranquillity and much delight
Are lost by counting, time and time again,
The small neglect, the unintended slight.
Grievances rust our spirits; let this, then,
Become our constant effort, to live quite
Above reproach both from, and to, all men.

Deliever us, O God, from the pride and self-love and self-will
that make us quick to resent small neglects and to suspect slights
where none has been intended. Help us, Father, if we have been
hurt by others' thoughtlessness, to be doubly careful not to hurt
others by our own. In Christ's name. AMEN.

One of the company said unto him, Master, speak to my brother, that he divide the inheritance with me.—Luke 12:13, K.J.V.

Martha was cumbered about much serving, and came to him, and said, Lord, dost thou not care that my sister hath left me to serve alone? bid her therefore that she help me.
—Luke 10:40, K.J.V.

LESSON FROM LUKE

When I grow critical, and quick at pointing
Out to another person his neglect
Of duty, and am angrily resentful
When he does not behave as I expect,
I think of one who came to Jesus, saying,
"Speak to my brother, Lord, that he divide
The inheritance with me." I think of Martha,
Fuming and fretting in her injured pride
At Mary's idleness, and saying, "Bid
Her therefore that she help me." I recall
That Christ rebuked the two complaining ones
And not the ones complained against at all.

And so I silence all my own complaining
And pray, "Speak to my brother, Lord, indeed,
And give him grace. But speak thou, most of all,
To me, and give the patience that I need."

Father in heaven, preserve us, we pray, from insisting that others be righteous only in our own way. Let us not censure others for following the guidance thou givest them, as we would follow what thou givest us. In Christ's name. AMEN.

Mary has chosen the good portion, which shall not be taken from her.
—Luke 10:42

MARY AND MARTHA

Mary:
I wasn't really idle, standing there
And looking at the maple's rosy bloom,
Soft, tender rose against the tender blue
Of the spring sky. Oh, how could I presume
Not to give thanks to God for it at once?
Should I have hurried on, and let God wait?
But while I prayed, the water boiled away,
And Martha's cross, because our tea is late.

Martha:
I saw the maple rosy-red with bloom,
Though Mary thinks I have no eyes at all,
And while I swept the walk, I thanked the Lord.
Should I have stood there, letting the broom fall
From idle hands while fifty duties waited—
My own, and Mary's too? what did she see
More than I saw? I've worked hard all this day,
And when I'm tired, I need my cup of tea.

Give us, dear Lord, the grace of knowing when to stop, lest frayed nerves and a criticizing temper be the price we pay for anxious industry. Save us from judging one another; help us to respect differences in personality, and to remember that few of us are ever wholly wrong or wholly right. In Christ's name we pray. Amen.

God is able to provide you with every blessing in abundance, so that you may always have enough of everything and may provide in abundance for every good work. —II Cor. 9:8

THE SAVERS

She saves scraps of paper
And gay cotton print
And gives understanding
And love, without stint.

She saves bits of string
And sunflower seed
And gives of herself
To any in need.

"It's good to be saving,"
She often will say.
"It's good to have something
For giving away."

God blesses the people
And lightens their lot
Whose heads are thrifty,
Whose hearts are not.

We thank thee, heavenly Father, for all the generous-hearted people who give of themselves, and who waste nothing that can be of use to others. We thank thee for those who save, in order to give. Forgive us, Lord, that we are often more concerned with our own desires than with other people's necessities. In Christ's name. AMEN.

Let all that you do be done in love. —I Cor. 16:14

IN ALL I DO

Creator of all,
While I create
Cookies to carry
On a sun-colored plate
To a quarrelsome neighbor,
And a gingerbread man
For a sick little boy
Who smiles when he can—

Creator of earth
And sky and sea,
Creator of love,
Abide in me,
And keep me aware
That in all I do
Creating love
I am one with you.

Creator and Father, we praise thee for the joyous privilege of doing things with thee. We praise thee, Lord of all, that every one of us in our own small and humble places may work with thee, if we do all our little tasks in love. Help us in all things to make love our aim, that we may abide in thee, and thou in us. Through Christ our Lord. AMEN.

And the effect of righteousness will be peace,
  and the result of righteousness, quietness and trust for ever.
My people will abide in a peaceful habitation,
  in secure dwellings, and in quiet resting places.

—Isa. 32:17-18

A NEW HOUSE MUST HAVE LOVE

A new house never seems to feel at home
On earth, until it has been loved sincerely
Through various weathers; with a feathery foam
Of snowdrift on its chimney, and as dearly
Engulfed in thunderous storms, or dusty-gray
With summer drought, as when spring sunlight blooms
In every shining window, or the gay
Gold radiance of October floods its rooms.

For any house with no experience
In facing tempests must have love, to give
Its harmony with earth, and confidence
In sky; a house assured of love will live
Contentedly at home with any weather,
And it and you will be at home together.

O God, who hast been our dwelling place in all generations, we thank thee for our earthly dwelling places. According to thy promise, Lord, let there be righteousness, and trust, and quietness, and peace within our hearts and within our homes. And may thy blessing be on all homes everywhere, making them places of abiding joy, and may all homeless people find peaceful habitations. AMEN.

Let us come into his presence with thanksgiving.—Ps. 95:2

THANKSGIVING TABLE

How joyously I offer praise for all
These loved hands folded now in thankfulness
In their familiar places; large and small
Well knowing in their own way how to bless.
Square little-boy hands, butterfly-deft ones
Of little girls, old hands whose touch instills
Quiet wisdom, strong hands warm with many suns,
And mother hands adept in tender skills—

Oh, I am thankful for the touch of these
Loved hands on mine, for all the wealth they hold
Of gentleness, and love, and healing ease,
And thankful, most of all, that all who fold
Their hands in reverential, thankful prayers
May feel the hand of God enfolding theirs.

We thank thee, gracious Father, for the joy that is ours when
loved ones who have been away return to us. Grant us deep aware-
ness of thy presence as we give thanks together for all thy blessings. And when we can no longer be together, but must go our
separate ways, be with each one of us and guide us constantly. We
pray in Christ's name. AMEN.

It is good to give thanks to the Lord,
*   to sing praises to thy name, O Most High;*
to declare thy steadfast love in the morning,
*   and thy faithfulness by night,*
. . . .
For thou, O Lord, hast made me glad by thy work;
*   at the works of thy hands I sing for joy.*

Ps. 92:1-2, 4

ONE DAY FOR THANKS

One day for giving thanks; and yet the sun
Sends abundant reassurance with each ray
Through all the year; and seed selects no one
Day's interval for growing want away
From earth; there is no stipulated hour
Alone of one brief season when eyes may see
The intricate slow opening of a flower
And the long rhythms of a wind-blown tree.

And since there are no set, specific times
When birds wake sudden music from still air
And childrens' lilting laughter soars and climbs,
How shall we set a time for thankful prayer?
How shall we pay, in one short interlude,
Our year-long debt of joyous gratitude?

Eternal Father, whose steadfast love never ceases, whose mercies never come to an end but are new every morning, renew our hearts each day to joy and praise. May we never lose the power of wonder, Lord, the power of marveling with delight at all thy works of faithfulness and love. In the name of Christ. AMEN.

THANKS FOR ALL

Lord, it is easy to give thanks for all
We have received and recognized as good,
But having given eager praise for small
And larger blessings, as they came, I would
Devote this day to thanking thee sincerely
For helping me through things that caused no thanks,
Through grave mistakes that hurt my heart severely
And failures that appeared but fortune's pranks.

I thank thee that I learned humility
From failures and mistakes, and that I grew
In patience and in confidence in thee
By every hard experience that I knew.
I thank thee, Father, now, with heart and will,
That thou wast with me, bringing good from ill.

Dear Lord, thou knowest that, in spite of thee, we all make many
blunders in words and in works. Give us the honesty and courage to
accept full responsibility for our mistakes, and to ask pardon of thee
and of those we wrong. We praise thee that thou art ever ready
to forgive and help us; we praise thee for all the help that thou
hast given. In Christ's name. AMEN.

Seek and you will find.—Matt. 7:7

THE SECRET

I seek for beauty everywhere
And see it where I seek.
It shines in sunny summer air
And beckons in the bleak
Bare bones of winter trees, on hills
Where splendor of a sunset spills.

It whispers in the winds that die
Along a dusky lane
Where pine trees pray, and cedars sigh
Their ageless, low refrain,
And it is in the little light
Of fireflies flitting through the night.

Oh, there is beauty singing
Wherever love may search,
In birds' wild onward winging,
And in a slender birch.
This is the secret that can dress
Sorrow itself in loveliness.

Lord of all beauty, keep us faithful, in the dark, unhappy days, to all that we have learned in times of joy. We thank thee that to those who seek for thee in times of sorrow thou givest beauty for ashes, the oil of joy for mourning, the garment of praise for the spirit of heaviness. For these gifts of thy love we praise thee in Christ's name. AMEN.

I am with you always.—Matt. 28:20

WAYFARING SONG

The path I walk may wander
Bewildered and forlorn
Through weeping ways of loneliness
And thistle sting and thorn;

But though the day be dreary
And though the night be long,
Through woeful ways and weary,
My heart shall keep a song.

My heart shall keep a singing
No storm or strife can still,
Though sore and steep the panting path
And perilous the hill;

For One shall walk beside me
Whose presence I may know
Whatever ill betide me,
So singing I shall go.

Dear Lord, we thank thee that thou art with us always, and that we need not despair when the way seems long and difficult. Keep us by thy grace from bitterness and rebellion, and from envying those whose way seems easier than ours. Oh, help us to walk the hard ways singing praises because thou art a God of steadfast love, in whom we trust forever. In Christ's name. AMEN.

He gives power to the faint,
  and to him who has no might he increases strength.
Even youths shall faint and be weary,
  and young men shall fall exhausted;
but they who wait for the Lord shall renew their strength,
  they shall mount up with wings like eagles,
they shall run and not be weary,
they shall walk and not faint.

—Isa. 40:29-31

AFTERWARD

After the worst has happened
With nothing more to fear,
The sun continues rising
With undiminished cheer,

And winds continue blowing
And skies continue fair,
As hearts continue bearing
The thing they could not bear.

Teach us, dear Lord, that if we are called upon to bear the things
we have thought we could not possibly bear, thou wilt strengthen
us to bear them. Give us, in our need, the love that bears all things
and endures all things, and is not irritable or resentful in distress
and suffering. In Christ's name. AMEN.

Do not be anxious about tomorrow.   —Matt. 6:34

IF FOR ONE DAY

If for one day
I can forget
The nagging care,
The needless fret;

For one day, keep
My spirit clear
From anxious doubt
And useless fear;

If for one day
I can believe
In life, and joyously
Receive

The blessings that
Are always mine
Of earth and air
And love divine—

Oh, then at last,
At last, I may
Learn how to do it
Every day.

Our heavenly Father, who knowest all our needs, forgive us our anxieties and fears. Sustain us day by day; keep us from all apprehensive concern about tomorrow. Let us be anxious only lest we may not be seeking thy righteousness first of all. Let thy peace possess our hearts and minds, through Christ. AMEN.

Where there is no vision, the people perish.
—Prov. 29:18, K.J.V.

REALITIES

This earth is sure
On which we live,
This absolute,
This positive,

Immediate earth,
The known, the near,
Confirming us
By being here

Beneath our feet;
And yet a star
Is no less real
For being far.

We thank thee, our Father, for starlike visions of love and truth and righteousness made manifest in our lives and in the lives of all people. Let us never doubt that every sincere effort we make in behalf of justice, mercy, and peace counts, even though the effort seems very small and though it seems to fail. Teach us, Lord, that it is the effort we make that matters, and help us to trust results to thee. In Christ's name. AMEN.

ASCENT

This is the hill I thought so high
I could not hope to reach its crest
However long I climbed; yet I
Have reached it now, and paused to rest
A moment, and, triumphant, view
The stones and briars I struggled past,
Unable to believe it true
That I have conquered them at last.

I cannot really catch a cloud
As I had half believed I could;
Attained, the height is not so proud
As I supposed, but it is good
Indeed to know that, having done
This, I can climb a taller one.

Father in heaven, we thank thee for high moments when some
good goal for which we have long struggled is attained. Grant that
we may never become satisfied with what we have done, but may
always seek for ways to serve thee better. May our desires and plans
be ever in harmony with thy will; so may we do all things through
Christ, who strengthens us. In his name. AMEN.

Day to day pours forth speech,
  and night to night declares knowledge.
                                    —Ps. 19:2

THE BEAUTY OF THE WHOLE

It is a thing most lovely to recall,
Most gracious, most deserving of our praise
And gratitude, that as we fill each small
And transitory moment of our days
With all we may of quiet faith of soul,
And all we may of love, and joy, and good,
Our lives become a singing, ordered whole
More beautiful than we believed they could.

For as we daily live the truth, and grow
Obedient to the Father's holy will,
Our days will speak of him, our nights will show
The knowledge that we gain of him, until
Our days and nights proclaim with one accord
The knowledge and the glory of the Lord.

We praise thee, Lord, that thou who hast ordained the sun and moon and all the hosts of heaven art mindful of us and dost care for us. We praise thee that as we sincerely strive to obey thy law of love and to live with thee from day to day, our lives may reflect the ordered loveliness of thy creation. We praise thee in Christ's name. Amen.

IV. LOVE NEVER ENDS

Love never ends; as for prophecy, it will pass away; as for tongues, they will cease; as for knowledge, it will pass away. For our knowledge is imperfect and our prophecy is imperfect; but when the perfect comes, the imperfect will pass away. When I was a child, I spoke like a child, I thought like a child, I reasoned like a child; when I became a man, I gave up childish ways. For now we see in a mirror dimly, but then face to face. Now I know in part; then I shall understand fully, even as I have been fully understood. So faith, hope, love abide, these three; but the greatest of these is love. —I Cor. 13:8-13

LOVE NEVER ENDS

Even the tongue in which our Saviour taught
The perfect law of love, has passed away.
Only because the words he spoke were fraught
With love, do any learn that tongue today.
The knowledge wise Athenians heard and told
Has vanished like a distant requiem,
But still men's spirits are made strong and bold
By news of love that Paul declared to them.

These three alone abide; the faith that God
Is love; the steadfast hope that love at last
Shall waken in the hearts of men who plod
Dark hopeless ways, obscure and overcast;
And love that is their purpose, and transcends
All faith and hope, the love that never ends.

Our heavenly Father, we have learned that this life becomes worthwhile and meaningful only as we strive to build into it the eternal values of faith and hope and love. Help us to set our hearts upon the things that are eternal, through Christ our Lord. AMEN.

He has made everything beautiful in its time; also he has put eternity into man's mind. —Eccl. 3:11

BUT NOT TOO WELL

Love well the sun,
Love well the earth,
All miracles
Of bloom and birth;

All little rains
On tender grass,
All seeking winds
That softly pass;

All glories of
Gold morning light,
All dear tranquillities
Of night;

Love well the earth's
Enchanted spell,
But love, oh, love
It not too well.

For earth will die
And dies the sun.
Keep loves that live
When earth is done.

Eternal God, all thy creation speaks to us of thee, and yet we know that thy creation shall someday pass away. And thou, Lord, hast put eternity into our minds, so that we cannot be deeply satisfied with the temporal. Beyond all the beauty thou hast made we seek thee, Lord, and we seek by the grace of Christ to grow in the love for thee that shall never pass away. In his name. AMEN.

Heaven and earth will pass away, but my words will not pass away.—Matt. 24:35

NOTHING LOVELIER

The world is full of lovely things
And gentle sights to see.
There is delight in redbird wings
And peace in every tree,
And there is rapture in the rush
Of winds along the way
And healing in the holy hush
That softly seals the day.

Yet there is nothing lovelier
In all the world than words,
Not all the gentle winds that stir
Nor all the winging birds.
The trees their ancient peace impart
In accents ever dear,
But words can heal a wounded heart
And free a soul from fear.

We thank thee, our Father, for all words fitly spoken that have enriched our minds with beauty and strengthened them with power. We thank thee most of all for the words of Christ that shall never pass away, the words of eternal life that, believed and lived, free us from fear forever. May his word dwell in us richly, that whatever we do in word or deed we may do in his name. AMEN.

The Spirit of the Lord is upon me,
because he has anointed me to preach good news to the poor.
He has sent me to proclaim release to the captives
and recovering of sight to the blind,
to set at liberty those who are oppressed.

—Luke 4:18

FOR MANY MAIMED

Oh, it is joy and rapture, ecstasy,
To hear earth's daily songs, see daily glow
Of light on all earth's beauties, and to go
In strength of wholeness, effortless and free.
Yet they, the inmates of catastrophe,
The deaf, the blind, the lame, enfeebled, slow,
Build goodly lives without the power to know
How good it is to run, to hear, to see.

Senses are tools for living, not the life.
Intrinsic life, denied them, may erect
Structures of living no least weakness mars.
The lone equipment of will's naked knife
Constructs strong habitations that protect
Or tall cathedrals soaring to the stars.

Our heavenly Father, we thank thee for the courage of all who live not by might or by power but by thy Spirit. We pray that thou wilt strengthen and sustain all who have been mutilated in body and soul by war, and all who are disabled by accident or illness. Grant that they may forgive those who are responsible for their suffering; save them from bitterness, and enable them to live victoriously. In Christ's name. AMEN.

She has been a helper of many.—Rom. 16:2

THE NURSE

Sometimes it seemed a weary thing to do
To rise each day in darkness, and to go
Through bitter weather to a patient who
Seemed often not to care, or even know,
When she arrived. It was no easy thing
To leave her own perplexities behind
And wear a tranquil, smiling face, to bring
Warm reassurance, comforting and kind.

But she had never studied how to spare
Her heart, or give her sympathy by measure,
And so one day her gentle, skillful care
Brought unexpected words for her to treasure,
"I knew I would be well—it's hard to say—
If I could live until you came, each day."

O God, we thank thee for those to whom thou hast given the gift of healing hands and healing hearts. We thank thee for those who, dealing daily with pain and misery, do not grow hardened to it but remain warmly concerned with each suffering individual. Increase our appreciation, Father, of the great value of such human service, and by thy grace sustain all who offer it to those in need. In Christ's name. AMEN.

Esteem them very highly in love because of their work.
—I Thess. 5:13

BENEFACTOR

Today I was made happier to learn
About a fellow citizen of mine
Who keeps a fleet of wheel chairs, not to earn
Reward for him—he has no such design—
But merely for the satisfaction he
Derives from loaning wheel chairs to the many
Folk who, without his thoughtfulness, would be
In need, without the means of having any.

I do not need a wheel chair, but I do
Need reassurance, when events would steal
Away my faith in kindness, and it grew
In strength today; and always, when I feel
Belief in selfless goodness growing dim,
I shall be glad, indeed, to think of him.

We thank thee, heavenly Father, for every example of unselfish service to others that increases our faith in human goodness. We thank thee for all people who do their good deeds in secret, avoiding the knowledge and praise of men, and all reward except the satisfaction of doing good. We pray thy blessing on them always. In Christ's name. AMEN.

Let your light so shine before men, that they may see your good works and give glory to your Father who is in heaven.

—Matt. 5:16

LANTERNS AND LAMPS

My parents carried light with them, for they
Lived in the days when people made their own
Or did without. The lantern's frosty ray,
When Dad came late from milking, always shone
As if a star were coming home to us,
And if I called at midnight, goblin-harried,
The shadows fled and night grew luminous
Before the little lamp that Mother carried.

Folk have small need of lamps and lanterns now;
Even on farms the darkness will withdraw
By swift electric magic, but somehow
I always shall be grateful that I saw
My parents' coming make the darkness bright
And knew them as the carriers of light.

Father of lights, we thank thee for all parents who are carriers of light. We thank thee that when we were children, and thought and reasoned like children, thou gavest us loving parents to comfort our fears and to bring light to us. For our parents' tender concern for us, and for all the goodness of their lives, we thank thee, Lord. In Christ's name. AMEN.

THE WILLOW ROAD

How many times we traveled
The weeping-willow road,
My Dad and I together,
Carrying a load

Of peaches to the market,
Of peas, or beans, or corn—
I must have started traveling it
As soon as I was born.

We'd ride along together
And both of us were shy
And neither of us mentioned
The weeping-willow sky,

The green and tremulous mystery
We traveled under all
The way into the city;
But though I don't recall

A word I said about it
Or one he said to me,
I like a weeping willow
As well as any tree.

We thank thee, Lord, for all memories of good hours spent with those whom we loved best. We thank thee for times of harmonious sharing of some experience, for times of quiet understanding that had no need of any words. We thank thee for all of our loved ones' love and wisdom that have become part of our lives. In Christ's name. AMEN.

I have fought the good fight, I have finished the race, I have kept the faith. —II Tim. 4:7

FOR MY FATHER

The silent strength of hills was his, the constant,
The necessary, changeless presence, grown
So usual in unobtrusive giving
Of strength, that we believed his strength our own.

And the enduring certitudes of earth
Were his, the richness time could not despoil.
Our lives were rooted in his deep assurance
As trees are rooted in essential soil.

Without him, though we trust that his eternal
Faith is fulfilled and his long task approved,
We bear within our hearts the desolation
Of mountains fallen and of earth removed.

Our heavenly Father, thou knowest the desolation of our hearts when those we love are no longer here with us. Yet in all our desolation, Father, we thank thee that we need not sorrow as those who have no hope. Help us, even in our deepest grief, to give thee thanks for their love for us and our love for them, and to know steadfastly that love never ends. In our Saviour's name. AMEN.

Neither death, nor life, nor angels, nor principalities, nor things present, nor things to come, nor powers, nor height, nor depth, nor anything else in all creation, will be able to separate us from the love of God in Christ Jesus our Lord. —Rom. 8:38

GRANDMOTHER'S MESSAGE

"Give my love to Laura,
Give my love to Jim."
Wherever Gramp was going,
Gran sent her love by him.

"Give my love to Susan,
Give my love to Todd."
Last night she whispered, gently,
"Give my love to God."

Eternal God, we thank thee for all people who through the heights and depths of troubled years are never too busy, perplexed, or sorrowful to give their love. We thank thee, Father, for the unending influence for good of lives that are lived in love, and we rejoice that nothing in all creation can separate such lives from thee. Through Christ our Lord. AMEN.

For this perishable nature must put on the imperishable, and this mortal nature must put on immortality. When the perishable puts on the imperishable, and the mortal puts on immortality, then shall come to pass the saying that is written:
  "Death is swallowed up in victory."   —I Cor. 15:53-54

CAUSE

Without the night
We could not dream
How beautifully
A star may gleam.

Without the dark
We could not know
How tenderly
A moon may glow.

And without death
We could not guess
How immortality
May bless.

We see as in a mirror dimly, Father; we know in part and understand in part, but we know that whether we live or die, we live and die unto thee. We see stars shining in the darkness and the glow of moonbeams in the night. We perceive the glory of the risen Christ. And we trust thee, Father, now and forevermore. AMEN.

And when they had sung a hymn, they went out to the Mount of Olives. —Matt. 26:30

BEFORE GETHSEMANE

"And then, when they had sung a hymn, they went
Out to the Mount of Olives." Let us keep
These words within our spirits, to prevent
Sighing and grumbling when our way seems steep.
The lonely agony, with friends who lay
In slumber while he suffered, the great wrong
Of one who kissed him only to betray—
Our Master went to meet them with a song.

Oh, let us sing, remembering hymns that rang
Down through the ages; let us not forget
That Paul and Silas, in their prison, sang
At midnight, praise to God; and, always, let
Us hold in radiant, reverent memory
That Jesus sang, before Gethsemane.

Give us, our God, the gift of singing spirits. Forgive us that, for-
getting that Christ sang before his betrayal, we think our troubles
are too great to meet with song; and forgive us that they ever seem
too small and trivial to call forth the best that is in us. Help us to
sing thy praises, Father, in troubles great and small, because of
Christ our Lord. AMEN.

Then he said to them, "My soul is very sorrowful, even to death; remain here, and watch with me." . . . And again he came and found them sleeping. —Matt. 26:38, 42-43

GETHSEMANE

My God, my God, my God,
Is all in vain?
Can these dull hearts learn love
From all my pain?

Was it too great, too vast,
The dream we dreamed,
Of all men saved by love,
All men redeemed?

Can even the Cross enlarge
Their hearts until they learn
To love with that pure love
For which we yearn?

Love is forever love.
Since thou art love, I wait
The fierceness of their rage,
The cruelty of their hate.

And it is not in vain
I drink this cup, if one,
If even one, learns love.
Thy will be done.

O God, enlarge our hearts to comprehend the greatness of Christ's suffering and the unsearchable depths of his love. Forgive us that we are more often asleep than awake to what he desires of us. Quicken us, for thy mercy's sake. AMEN.

Now from the sixth hour there was darkness over all the land until the ninth hour. —Matt. 27:45

GOOD FRIDAY

Today no lily blooms,
No sparrrow sings.
Folded their petals all,
Folded their wings,

Since He who gave them flower
And gave them song
Hangs on the fearful cross
Of bitter wrong.

A darkness on the land,
Thick darkness everywhere.
No bud, no wing can stir
This heavy air.

Men have destroyed all song,
Despoiled all flower,
Delivering all life
To death's dark power.

But purer songs shall soar,
And purer bloom
When Christ's eternal life
Destroys the tomb.

Lord God of love, make brave our hearts to look upon the cross where love was crucified. We are appalled by it, O God of all. We wish that there had been some easier way. Teach us that love does not seek the easy way. Let us never seek escape from his cross, or from ours, that we may not betray him, or deny him. In his name. AMEN.

Mary stood weeping outside the tomb. . . . Jesus said to her, "Mary."
—John 20:11, 16

MARY AT THE TOMB

What pain tormented her all night,
What seven demons of despair
Relived the crucifying sight
With sneering leer and mocking glare
We are not told. Pale morning light
Shone on the stone and found her there.

Though love lay slain in alien tomb
And faith seemed false, and truth untrue,
And doubt and death were all her doom,
One deed of love remained to do.
She brought rich spices through the gloom,
And turned; and saw the Lord they slew.

So all who rise from nights of dread and fear
To little acts of love may find him near.

O merciful and gracious God our Father, we thank thee in overwhelming wonder for the resurrection miracle. In deepest reverence we thank thee, Lord, for Christ victorious over death and evil, for Mary's weeping turned to utmost joy. Oh, keep us faithful in our times of darkness, that we too may find him near us in the gloom. In his name. AMEN.

When he was at table with them, he took the bread and blessed, and broke it, and gave it to them. And their eyes were opened and they recognized him; and he vanished out of their sight.

—Luke 24:30-31

FOREVER IN THEIR HEARTS

They walked the road to Emmaus together,
Two men with anxious, troubled hearts, and One
So perfectly at peace, they questioned whether
He understood their sorrow. Till the sun
Descending bade them pause for food and rest,
They walked and talked with him. Then at the board
The tranquil Stranger broke the bread, and blessed
And gave; and so they recognized their Lord.

Instantly then he vanished. Never grieve
For them, bereft, nor say men ever learn
The truth too late, and lose as they receive.
Forever in their hearts that truth shall burn.
Those who have walked with him, and known one white
Moment of vision, have no more need of sight.

O giving God, we thank thee that it was in blessing and in giving that Christ was made known to the disciples. Help us, who strive to follow him, always to bless and give. Grant, our Father, that Christ may dwell in our hearts by faith, that we, being rooted and grounded in love, may comprehend the love of Christ that passes knowledge, and be filled with all the fullness of God. AMEN.

The Lord is risen indeed.—Luke 24:34 K.J.V.

HE IS RISEN

The Lord is risen indeed! We know it true,
Since we, who cannot see him at our side,
Have as abundant proof as had the two
Who walked with him until the eventide.
For we have witnessed fear-tormented men
Transformed, like Peter, to men who boldly dare
All things for Him, and women now, as then,
Saved, even as Mary, from extreme despair.

No surer proof than this could anyone
Require. By every burden bravely borne,
By every selfless act of service done,
By every kindness in return for scorn,
By every swift response to human need,
We know that Christ the Lord is risen indeed.

Our heavenly Father, most earnestly we pray that the grace of the
risen Christ may fill our minds and souls, inspiring us to works of
faithful love, that our lives may testify that he is risen indeed. In
his name. AMEN.

It is the God who said, "Let light shine out of darkness," who has shone in our hearts to give the light of the knowledge of the glory of God in the face of Christ.   —II Cor. 4:6

BEYOND THE STAR

I looked long at a star,
Deeply, and long,
Till suddenly I looked beyond the star
For one transcendent instant, and caught a glimpse
Of God.

And now I go with astonishment in my heart
And sorrow,
Knowing that the earth is too narrow,
And the sky too low,
And the souls of men too small
To contain so much vastness
Of love.

God,
Help us grow.

O God, who hast called us out of darkness into thy marvelous light, we thank thee for all vivid realizations of thy great, surpassing love. We thank thee for moments when thou shinest deep into our hearts, illuminating them. May the radiance of such moments remain with us through all the joys and sorrows of our days, helping us to attain to the stature of the fullness of Christ. In his name. AMEN.